Emotional Intelligence

Simple Ways To Fix Your EQ

By Alex Canny

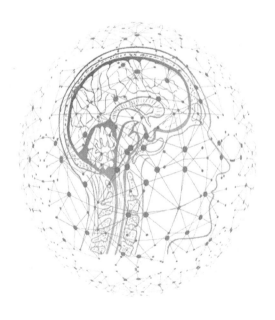

Table of Contents

COPYRIGHT

Introduction

Is emotional intelligence as crucial as intellectual intelligence for success and improving your quality of life? Can your emotional intelligence quotient enhance your quality of relationships and give you a contented life? Well, the answer is yes – in fact, it may be more significant than intellectual intelligence! The concept of emotional intelligence has evolved over the years, and it is important to know how it has evolved from being known as social intelligence in the 1930s to emotional strength in the middle of 20th century to today's jargon - emotional intelligence.

So, what is emotional intelligence and why is it so important? Why do you think experts have begun to ask people to work on their emotional intelligence for both personal and professional growth? Studies and surveys show that people who have a high level of emotional intelligence find it easier to manage both their personal and professional lives equally well. They can succeed at work, build stronger and healthier relationships, and accomplish personal and professional goals with ease.

When you can identify, understand, manage and use your emotions in positive ways to rise above challenges, communicate efficiently, alleviate stress, neutralize conflicts and empathize with others, your emotional intelligence is perfect! Do you think emotional intelligence is essential only for people who work in fields that require active communication with the others? Yes? That's not true! Emotional intelligence isn't restricted to a specific work area or people – it is required for everyone. It is the perfect gateway for a well-balanced life in every aspect!

The way you interact with people, the way you behave with your colleagues, the way you respond to strangers or the way you handle stress – emotional intelligence impacts every aspect of your regular day-to-day life. If your emotional intelligence is high, you are fortunate enough to:

- *Identify your emotional state*

- *Analyze and understand the emotional states of people around you*

- *Engage yourself with people in a way that they are drawn to you*

When you can understand the emotions of people, you can use it to empathize, help, achieve and succeed. How do you do it? You will be in a better position to relate to people and situations, work toward healthy relationships both in the personal and professional area, attract success towards self and lead a contented life.

It is a well-known fact that the smartest or brightest people are not always successful in their personal lives – even academically brilliant people might not be successful in their personal lives or professional setups. IQ doesn't always guarantee success in life! Yes, it can help you get a job or into college, but to survive and battle your stress and emotions in those situations, you will need EQ.

Today, you often hear the term Emotional Intelligence in business meetings, within your human resource department and in executive boardrooms. Companies prefer people who are people-smart rather than book-smart. A particular survey conducted by a job site found that almost one-third of employers have started to emphasize hiring and promoting people with emotional intelligence, especially after the recession era.

Chapter 1: What Is Emotional Intelligence

Emotions. They can be a very powerful force in our lives.

Because it is so powerful that it makes emotional intelligence one of the most valuable assets we could cultivate for ourselves. Emotional intelligence is simply the ability to identify, manage and regulate your own emotions. It is also about being able to identify the emotions of others around you, and what you do with that information you receive. Emotional intelligence is about your ability to capitalize on these emotions and use them to your best advantage.

THE 5 CORE PRINCIPLES OF EMOTIONAL INTELLIGENCE

Emotional intelligence can essentially be summed up in two ways - the ability to recognize, understand and manage your emotions, and the ability to influence the emotions of others. Emotional intelligence into five core principles:

- *Self-awareness*

- *Self-regulation*

- *Motivation*

- *Empathy*

- *Social skills*

THESE FIVE CORE principles are the qualities that everyone with high EQ should possess. This is going to be the framework that you are going to work towards as you work on mastering self-awareness and controlling your emotions.

SELF-AWARENESS

How aware are you about the state of your emotions? Do you recognize them as they happen? Or do you only notice how emotional you were after you've had some time to look back and reflect on your actions? As you learn to master self-awareness, EQ is going to teach you how to recognize your emotions as they happen, how to tune in and be mindful towards what you're experiencing. EQ will teach you how to recognize the effects that your emotions have, and what to do about them.

Self-Regulation

Having an awareness of your emotions alone is not going to be enough. It is what you do with them that matters just as much. Are you going to let your emotions control you? Or are you going to be the one who is in control? It is easy to lose control when you don't know how to regulate your emotions, especially when they first happen. This is why self-regulation is an important step in the EQ process because it teaches you to be adaptable and flexible in handling changes. It teaches you to take responsibility for your actions, and it helps keep you in check, so you don't give in to your disruptive impulses.

Motivation

Motivation is what gives you a sense of achievement to keep on pushing forward. To constantly push yourself to be even better. To strive for high levels of excellence and to have the initiative needed to act on opportunities that present themselves. These are qualities which are displayed by a lot of successful and influential leaders. Do you notice how they always have the optimism needed to keep pursuing their goals despite the curveballs and challenges that life throws at them? That's because they've got high levels of emotional intelligence. It keeps them going to accomplish the task and the goals that they have committed themselves to while remaining optimistic in the process. They never think about quitting because they have trained their minds always to see things from a positive perspective. They've trained themselves to see the silver lining in every situation, and they have reprogrammed their minds to focus on solving the problem at hand.

Empathy

Empathy helps emotionally intelligent individuals recognize and anticipate the needs of another individual. They then use this ability to work on fostering and building powerful relationships with a diverse group of people. Because they have the capacity to identify the needs and wants of another person, they can decipher the feelings of others, sometimes even preventing conflict before it happens because they can sense what's brewing underneath the surface. The more you can decipher the feelings of people, the better you can manage the thoughts and approaches you send them.

Social Skills

Emotionally intelligent people make such successful leaders because they are able to inspire and guide groups of individuals. They have the ability to develop good interpersonal skills, and it is these people skills which allow them to negotiate, understand and empathize with others. Their social skills help them to form meaningful bonds with a diverse group of people, especially in a work environment. They can easily influence others with their effective, persuasive techniques. They are seen as a catalyst for change because they have developed their social skills to a point where they are seen as influential and likable individuals.

THESE FIVE CORE principles are the reason why emotionally intelligent people are so successful at what they do. This is how they rise to the top, to become the affluent leaders that others look up to. It isn't a skill that they were born with. It is a skill that they cultivate for themselves over time and practice. EQ is a skill that you too, are going to learn to master by the time you reach the end of this guidebook.

The Qualities of People with High Emotional Intelligence

It isn't just academic intelligence that runs the world we live in. In fact, it takes a combination of several factors and intelligence types to accomplish true success — one of them is emotional intelligence. The term that is used to measure a person's intelligence is called the quotient.

SOME EXAMPLES of quotients include IQ (intelligence quotient), which is focused on one's ability to memorize and retrieve information from memory and logical reasoning which is also known as being academically brilliant. The emotional quotient (EQ or emotional intelligence) on the other hand, is focused on one's ability to manage, understand and recognize not just their own emotions, but the emotions of the people around them too.

OUR EMOTIONS MAKE up a large part of who we are. We are emotional, and sometimes we respond according to those emotions. We even make decisions based on those emotions. Having emotional intelligence is just as important - if not more- to a person's success. Not only will you be able to manage and regulate your own emotions, but you can learn to influence the minds of the people around you too, as you learn to master and become better at EQ.

IT IS easy to spot someone with high EQ, and if there are people around you that you can use as examples of what to strive for, that's going to be a big help. Essentially, when someone displays any of the following qualities below, it is a safe bet to say that they've got high levels of emotional intelligence:

•   *They Have a High Sense of Self-Awareness* - A person with high EQ has a very clear idea of how they perceive themselves, and how others around them perceive them. Someone with high EQ has mastered the art of self-awareness to the point that they completely understand themselves and how they work. They understand what factors trigger their emotions and they have learned how to manage themselves in the most proactive manner possible. They are also not afraid to seek out honest feedback from others, and they welcome constructive criticism because it helps them develop a better understanding of themselves.

•   *They're Emphatic Towards Others* - A person with high EQ has the ability to relate to the people around them in a way that many others do not. They have a strong sense of empathy, and they use that quality to see things from another person's perspective. To truly understand how someone feels, you need to be able to walk a mile in their shoes, as the saying goes. This quality is exactly what helps them mirror someone else's emotions and feelings, to feel what they feel. It enables them to understand what the person is going through emotionally. This is a skill which they have cultivated through practice and experience.

•   *They Are Curious Creatures* - They are always on the lookout for ways they can improve, and they're ever ready to learn something new. Curiosity is one of the key traits that you need to achieve success because successful people never stop learning and growing. They are passionate about life and knowledge, and they are driven every day to look for ways to become a better version of themselves. People with high EQ are always curious, and this leads to them never wanting to stop learning.

• *Their Mind Works in Analytical Ways* - People with high EQ don't just receive information and leave it at that. On the contrary, what they do instead is process and analyze the information that they receive on a deeper level. Emotionally intelligent individuals are deep thinkers, and they are always analyzing how information can be improved on and what could be done better. This is part of what makes them such great leaders, to begin with. They are problem solvers, and they always think about the why behind a certain action. They think about what benefit that course of action brings, and if this is the best scenario for everyone involved.

• *They Think Positive* - This isn't just another cliche saying for emotionally intelligent individuals. In fact, they are the living embodiment of this aspect. Despite the obstacles and challenges that come their way, those who possess high EQ maintain an optimistic attitude because they know how important it is for the mind to maintain this level of positivity. If they allow themselves to wallow in self-pity and let themselves be consumed by negative emotions and desires, they know it is only a matter of time before things quickly spiral out of control, as it often does when negativity takes over. Being optimistic and positive is the only way to keep increasing the opportunities and improve the relationships that come their way constructively and productively.

Chapter 2: Identifying Your Own Emotions

Start the first day by knowing yourself completely. Being self-aware is the cornerstone of emotional intelligence. When you are self-aware, you identify your own emotions and become more mindful of them on a minute to minute basis, thus recognizing the feelings created by these emotions and the ability to manage them in the best possible manner.

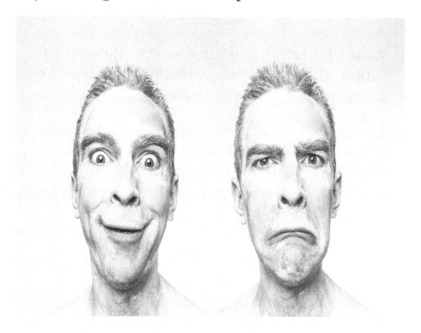

People who are self-aware will seldom be overpowered by their emotions. When you know how you think and feel, it is easier to understand your entire emotional framework and stop being a victim of your own destructive emotions. You hold complete control over how you respond to any situation. This leads to greater self-assurance and the ability to form mutually beneficial relationships.

Here's how to develop greater self-awareness:

Day 1: Journaling

Journaling is a wonderful way to gain deeper insights into one's thoughts, feelings, and emotions at the beginning or end of each day or anytime during the day, actually. It's like taking stock of your emotions the way you would take an inventory of physical products.

Write what exactly you felt when something specific happened during the day, including physiological reactions, sensations (faster heartbeat, sweating, dizziness, etc.), and more.

I personally like to make a list of roles that I actively fulfill on an everyday basis. For instance, parent, partner, co-worker, gym buddy, etc. What are your feelings towards each role at the end of the day?

You may be a very content parent but a frustrated professional. Similarly, you can be a happy spouse but an anxious businessperson. From day one onward, think of each important role and your feelings towards the role. When you identify your own feelings for every role, you get more power in controlling those emotions towards that specific role. It will not just increase your understanding of your feelings towards that role but also put you in control of your own feelings and emotions when it comes to that relationship.

Day 2: Do a Mental Check-In

Do what pesky yet well-meaning house-keepers and guest services personnel do at hotels. They knock on the door and keep asking you if you need anything. Similarly, you knock on your mental door (without really saying, "Do you need cleaning services or perhaps some tea or coffee?") and tap into how you are feeling at any given point. You can actually do this multiple times a day. Take a complete account of your emotions. Where are those feelings originating from? Why are you feeling the way you are feeling? What physical signs indicate those feelings? Do your feelings and emotions follow in quick succession? Are they accompanied by physical sensations? Are these emotions visible through your body language (expressions, gesture, leg movements, posture)? Are your feelings easily noticed by others? Are your decisions driven by your emotions? Even though it is a near impossible exercise, try to observe your emotions in a neutral and non-judgmental manner.

For instance, if you don't agree with a co-worker about something, try to delve deep into the reasons. What has prompted your disagreement? Are you genuinely in disagreement with the point raised by your co-worker, or is it simply a clash of egos? Are you simply envious of the person or dislike him or her because of some reason that leads to your disagreement with one another?

Professional sportspeople are offered intensive training in emotional intelligence. Yes, a sport is a competition of physical prowess, but the attitude of competitiveness, handling stress, overcoming obstacles, and winning begins in the mind. During crucial events, when an athlete can identify and manage his emotions in the best possible manner, it impacts their performance and chances of winning dramatically. Similarly, their performance is not negatively affected by their feelings and emotions.

When you are fully aware of your feelings and emotions, you know your strengths and weaknesses. These realistic expectations give you greater confidence and leave little room for disappointment. This eventually leads to greater overall social adaptability and competency.

When you gain greater awareness of your own and other people's feelings, you don't become a prisoner of emotions. There is a greater control over your responses, which increases your sense of self-worth.

Labeling your emotions is another fine way to run through your emotional experiences. This helps people in several ways, including recognizing fundamental triggers of specific negative emotions. Whenever you feel the need to identify what causes you to think or act in a certain way, write down the precise emotion of your experience. As much as possible, you must also include what triggered the emotion.

For instance, what makes you angry towards a particular person? Is it something to do with the way they are as a person or your own low self-esteem or self-assuredness?

Or is it to do with a bias that has been deeply ingrained into you by society? Be honest and write down what triggers specific destructive emotions in you. Once you recognize triggers, it is easier to manage or respond to those triggers.

Sometimes you may hate a person simply because you believe they have a better life than you, and what you could be experiencing may be nothing more than jealousy pangs.

When you identify the feelings as jealousy, you are in a better position to deal with these potentially damaging emotions. Labeling gives you the right perception to develop a clearer understanding of your emotions. Thus, we can manage our responses or reactions in a more constructive manner.

Also, pay attention to physical clues when it comes to identifying your emotions. By getting into the habit of listening to your body, you will realize that your body can tell you a lot about how your mind is feeling.

Our physical and mental selves are more entwined than we believe. They have a profound impact on each other. When you pick physical signals from the body, you'll get a clue about your emotions too. For instance, if there's a knot in your stomach, or your breathing pace quickens, or the chest feels rigid, you may be stressed or nervous. Sadness makes your limbs slow and heavy, and it takes a lot of effort to walk down even a few steps. Similarly, extreme joy and nervousness increases your heartbeat and gives you butterflies in the stomach.

You are simply identifying your emotions and not judging them. All emotions, whether negative or positive, are valid. Judging our emotions is not recommended because it will unnaturally inhibit the manner in which these emotions are expressed.

Treat each new emotion like a new piece of information linked closely with what is happening inside your mind. You will be at a loss about how to react appropriately without connecting with your inner self. This is exactly why the power to identify and manage your emotions is a type of intelligence which is sometimes believed to be even more important than regular intelligence quotient. Experience both positive and negative emotions and learn from them. Even if you are feeling an intensely negative emotion, it will tell you something about the situation.

I'd go a step further and state or name your emotions. Research in the field of neuroscience and neuro-linguistics suggests that naming your emotions is one of the simplest yet most effective ways to reduce its intensity.

What you are doing is taking the spotlight away from the emotion and thinking about emotions in a cognitive manner. Another trick is to speak about your emotions as a third person. For instance, instead of saying, "I am annoyed," try saying, "John is annoyed." If that appears too weird or freaky, try, "I am undergoing a feeling of annoyance or irritation." It leads to neutralizing intense emotions and acts as a more soothing mechanism. Treat your emotions as some sort of information or knowledge rather than something that needs to be resolved right away.

Name your compelling emotions and let the emotions last for a few seconds without giving in to the urge of reacting to them. Just feel them for a while without doing anything about it. Allow yourself to feel angry, jealous, frustrated, annoyed and pretty much anything else that you are feeling. The more you try to push out or stop feeling something, the more these feelings will bounce back. According to physiological research, it takes around six seconds for our body to absorb emotion-related chemicals.

Day 3: Mindfulness

Mindfulness is another brilliant way to gain self-awareness at any given time. While some people recommend setting aside a fixed time for meditation, I'd say you can even practice it during a quick coffee break. Mindfulness is about developing a connection with your deeper, inner self. It is about enhancing your intuition or your ability to tune in to what your inner self is trying to communicate with feelings and emotions. You train yourself to "listen" to your feelings and emotions as they occur in the present without judging them. When a consistent mindfulness practitioner develops the habit of identifying feelings as they originate, he or she gains priceless insight about their emotions, which ultimately helps in resolving several pressing issues.

Mindfulness teaches you to be in the moment and identify emotions as they occur. How to meditate or practice mindfulness?

Nothing fancy. Just sit on a chair or the ground in a comfortable posture. Use support (if required) in the form of pillows. Close your eyes. Start by focusing on your breath. Notice everything from the sensation of the air entering your lungs to the process of exhaling. Clear your mind from all regrets of the past and anticipations of the future. Eliminate all stressful situations from the mind. Your mind should be a blank slate that includes no feelings and emotions. Count from 1-4 each time you inhale, and then four counts again when you exhale. Keep the breath slow and focused. Don't focus your thoughts on what is beyond your control. Rather, focus only on the breath by calming your thoughts. Even if your thoughts wander, bring them gently back to the breath.

Another way is to breathe by counting 1, followed by breathing out at the count of 1. Slow down a bit and now inhale at two counts (1-2) and exhale at two counts. Next, make it even more relaxed and slow it down to 1-3, and eventually 1-4. Repeat in a pattern you are comfortable with.

Observe how your lungs feel when a fresh supply of oxygen reaches them. How does the throat feel when air passes through it? How does your stomach feel?

Mindful meditation helps build tremendous self-awareness. When you meditate, you gain the ability to reflect on your actions without being affected by them. Reflection helps you connect with yourself and developer higher self-awareness. Find a calm, undisturbed corner in your home (or workplace) and devote time to an activity that helps you get in touch with your inner self.

Mindfulness is essentially a Buddhist practice that is great for concentrating all attention on the present.

Daily mindfulness induces a sense of calmness, which is ideal when it comes to recognizing feelings and emotions in an objective manner and manages them more efficiently by gaining a better perspective of the situation.

When you come to appreciate the present, you develop a calmer and more focused mindset that is ideal for making decisions or reacting. You learn to tune in to every sensation and emotion to gather a better perspective on life. When you are tempted to respond, you learn to think through your emotions in an objective manner and get a firm hold over them.

Mindfulness can be practiced in several ways, including mindful eating, driving, or walking. Observe your emotions while going out for a walk all by yourself or while eating a meal alone.

All our emotional experiences also impact us physically at some level though we aren't always aware of it. When we become emotionally tense, our bodies instinctively react on a more primordial level in response to a threat. It's an involuntary chemical reaction where our blood vessels contract, the heart rate increases, and our breathing becomes more rapid.

However, this reaction to stress can be calmed if we reduce the emotional stress quickly. Each time you feel emotionally stressed, take a deep and slow breath. Breathe gradually and deeply. Focus on allowing the air to circulate in and out of the abdomen. Do this for a while, and you'll feel like there is a fresher batch of oxygen entering your body. The chemical reactions in the body will put you in an indisputably better state of mind before you begin interacting with others or face a potentially stressful situation.

Even in social situations, train yourself to pay attention to physiological signs of emotions. There are consistent physical patterns connected with each of the six basic human emotions. Reduced sensations in the limbs can be an indication of intense sadness, or sensations felt in the digestive system can translate into a feeling of utter disgust. Similarly, rage leads to heightened sensations in the upper limb region. Surprise, anxiety, uncertainty, and fear lead to sensations in and around the chest area.

Mindfulness is a purposeful, non-judgmental way to appreciate the present and acknowledge your emotions without attempting to push them away. If you do feel fleeting emotions while practicing mindfulness, simply acknowledge it and move back to the focus of your attention without being overwhelmed by it.

Day 4: Get Feedback

How do you improve your performance in the workplace? You can do it through your annual appraisal, feedback, or evaluation session with your manager or with the human resources department. Together, you conduct an overview of your annual performance, while identifying strengths and areas for improvement.

Why can't this be applied to your personal or social life? Why not get trusted opinion from family and well-meaning friends? They can offer their candid and unbiased views to help you gain a straightforward perspective on your emotions. Let people know that you are looking for genuine, constructive, and straightforward feedback.

Don't get offended by genuine feedback offered by people. Listen to them without succumbing to the urge of reacting or justifying or rationalizing your acts. People should be comfortable giving you their unbiased opinion. Listen to their views carefully without filtering them. You can ask for honest feedback by saying something such as, "I trust your judgment completely which is why I am seeking an honest and unbiased opinion from you, is that alright?"

I also know someone who has appointed little soldiers within their group to call out their behavior when they are doing something they shouldn't or when there's something they want to change.

For example, if you have the habit of hogging the limelight at all social gatherings and genuinely want to give up the tag of an attention seeker, get someone to call out your behavior gently and personally each time they find you trying to hog the limelight. Let your family member or friend know that they have to discreetly point out the actions you wish to change. The same also applies to a professional set-up. Get your managers or other formal channels to regularly offer you constructive feedback. It helps you tap into your strengths and work upon your weaknesses to boost emotional intelligence and social skills. Get a 360-degree reality check on multiple core competency areas.

Self-awareness is never going to be a brief pursuit. It is a lifelong journey that will keep helping you when it comes to developing greater emotional intelligence and evolved social skills. Though self-awareness is a constant pursuit, the points mentioned above will put you on the right track.

Day 5: Observe the Connection Between Your Emotions and Actions

What is your reaction to overpowering emotions? What is your gut response to situations faced on a daily basis? The more efficiently you can identify what triggers your behavior, the greater your emotional quotient will turn out to be.

You'll know what you need to change your behavior pattern if you can establish a clear link between your emotions and actions. For example, when you feel embarrassed, uncomfortable, or insecure, you may withdraw from a conversation and go into a shell. Similarly, you may raise your voice each time you are angry or even walk out of a room. Some people start panicking or crying when they are nervous or overwhelmed. Understand the specific behavior that drives your emotion, which will help you wield more control over your actions.

Also, don't forget to celebrate positive emotions. Emotional intelligence is not just about identifying and managing challenging emotions. It is also about the power of celebrating positive emotions to attract even more of them. People who celebrate and experience positive emotions not only enjoy more fulfilling relationships but are also more resilient when it comes to responding to the not so positive emotions or events.

Purposefully do things that add more value to your life or make you happy. Small things like practicing gratitude or being thankful for all that you have, engaging in random acts of kindness, thinking about or visualizing positive experiences, eating healthy, and exercising can go a long way to putting you in a more positive frame of mind while thinking or interacting with others.

Chapter 3: Difference between Intelligence Quotient and Emotional Quotient

How does emotional quotient differ from intelligence quotient? The simple answer is- they measure different forms of intelligence. Your technical acumen or technical skills is a direct result of a high intelligence quotient. You've mastered your skills well, which is a reflection of well-developed cognitive abilities. However, is intelligent quotient enough to determine your success when it comes to dealing with people (unless you are cooped up on a remote island all yourself, you have to deal with people)?

While intelligence quotient measures your technical expertise, emotional quotient evaluates your ability to manage your and other people's emotions in your work and personal life. You know where every employee stands when it comes to technical prowess but do you really understand their thoughts, actions and feelings to be able to better manage your and their behavior in sync with these emotions. When we gain insights into the underlying emotional patterns of people, it becomes easier to relate to them and channelize more productive behavior. This is a fundamental difference between intelligence quotient and emotional quotient.

Ever wondered why some of the cleverest people hit a blank in their professional lives and just can't seem to climb the corporate ladder, while the less knowledgeable and inexperienced folks smoothly sail their way to professional success? We all know of people who don't exactly possess the slickest technical skills yet surprisingly manage to reach top management positions. What is it that sets them apart from their more technically competent peers? Emotional intelligence is the key. It is their ability to recognize and control their and other's emotions to build more productive relationships that helps them score.

A person's intelligence quotient demonstrates their core technical competencies, cognitive development and unusual abilities, their emotional intelligence determines their ability to identify emotions and deal with others. Your emotional quotient determines how you will deal with stress, difficult people, bullying, high pressure work situations, conflict within the team, and differences in relationships.

Intelligence is an indicator of your cognitive prowess such as logical thinking, analytical reasoning, memorizing information, solving problems, verbal abilities, creative thinking and much more. Emotional intelligence is controlling your and other's emotions for creating optimally positive circumstances. Starkly different from your ability to comprehend words and numbers, emotional quotient helps you develop healthy interpersonal relationships in your personal and work life.

Emotional intelligence can include stress management, intuition, emotional flexibility, empathy, honestly and more. Emotional quotient highlights your and others emotions with respect to changing circumstances and people, while intelligence quotient is all about cognitive abilities.

While intelligence quotient can determine your success during your academic stint, emotional quotient is vital for all round success in life. You may excel as a student if you possess a high intelligence quotient. However to attain overall success in life, you need a high emotional quotient.

Research has indicated that there are five fundamental skills that distinguish the star performers from low performers.

These skills are empathy, self-awareness, assertiveness, problem solving and happiness. Potential recruits who score high on these five attributes are 2.7 times likelier to succeed than folks who bag low scores.

So, why is emotional quotient so closely associated with a person's chances of becoming successful in life? The answer is – awareness of emotions and ability to express themselves confidently. Emotionally intelligent people are experts in gauging people's emotions and altering their pitches/presentations accordingly. Little wonder then that emotionally intelligence is so vital for people in sales, customer service, counseling and other industries.

For instance, a study closely followed the recruitment of sales personnel for cosmetic giant L'Oreal based on their emotional skills. It was observed that these emotionally competent sales people outdid other salespersons by a whopping $91,370 to amass a net revenue growth of $ 2,558, 360. In another research, a national insurance firm discovered that salespersons who were low on emotional skills like initiative, confidence and empathy sold far less policies (average premium of $54,000) that agents who scored high on emotional skills (average premium of $114,000). You get the picture, right? When you show high emotional competencies by being proactive, self confident and empathetic, you are able to connect to potential buyers and help them buy rather than simply sell.

In the workplace, intelligence quotient helps for analyzing, connecting the dots and undertaking research and development. Emotional intelligence is about forging a strong team spirit, leadership, building successful professional relationships, collaboration, service and initiative. Emotional quotient can be gained and enhanced as opposed to intelligence quotient, which is a more inborn and hereditary characteristic.

The goal for businesses isn't to simply hire people who are intellectually competent, but lack emotional or people skills. Today's competitive and social interactions dominated world demands workers who are smart (that's a given), and endowed with more thoughtfulness. The ideal candidate is a combination of emotional intelligence and general intelligence. Since all candidates applying for a position possess more or less the same technical competence, emotional intelligence often becomes a clinching factor when it comes to selecting people for important roles.

Standford-Binet, Woodcock-Johnson Tests of Cognitive abilities and Wechsler are some popular intelligence quotient tests, while Mayer-Salovey-Caruso Test and Daniel Goleman model score test are popular emotional intelligence assessment tests. An Intelligence Quotient test generally involves a collection of standardized questions where participants are assigned precise scores based on their answers. These scores are evaluated with respect to average scores within the age group to establish a person's intellectual capabilities.

Emotional quotient tests, on the other hand, are more challenging to administer because feelings and emotional skills are tougher to depict numerically. While intelligence quotient questions have a definite answer for every question, emotional quotient tests tend to be more subjective and require greater evaluation effort. Unlike IQ tests, there aren't any right or wrong answers. Respondents may not answer questions honestly simply to rank high or may adjust their responses according to what they are currently experiencing, which makes these results more skewed. There may be a tendency on part of the participant to say exactly what the evaluators want to hear rather than responding truthfully.

People possessing a high intelligence quotient are excellent at conducting tasks. They are quick absorbers of new skills and information. However, if they have a low emotional quotient, they tend to overlook their and others feelings. For instance, when something doesn't turn out according to the way they wanted, these folks tend to lose their temper and lash out at people. While someone who is high on emotional intelligence will learn to control their emotions and get along with people around them. They are extremely effective when it comes to working as a team or working in a leadership role.

The concept of emotional intelligence has gained such a strong momentum that it has impacted a large a large number of areas including the corporate world. Several top organizations have now made emotional intelligence tests mandatory as part of the hiring process, along with intelligence quotient.

In personal relationships, 90 percent of the issues arise due to lack of emotional intelligence. Everything revolves around empathy, self awareness, awareness of the other person's emotions, understanding, communication patterns and the likes, which are all components of emotional intelligence.

Emotional quotient is not the antithesis of intelligence quotient. They aren't mutually exclusive. Some folks possess both in huge quantities, while others possess neither. Psychologists are keener to explore how the two attributes balance each other. For instance, how your ability to deal with stress impacts your ability to focus or learn new information.

Chapter 4: Benefits of Emotional Intelligence

As discussed earlier, emotional intelligence is our ability to manage our and other's emotions by discriminating among these feelings, and using the information to guide our words, thoughts and actions. To cut a long story short, emotional intelligence is an aggregation of your mental and emotional skills. Emotionally intelligent people enjoy a multitude of benefits in all spheres of life including relationships, career and social life. Here are some ways in which your life can be impacted or benefited if you consciously focus on developing high emotional intelligence.

Stellar Productivity

Emotional intelligence has a high correlation with an individual's work performance. Research has revealed that emotional intelligence is twice as crucial as technical/cognitive abilities even among professions such as engineering. Emotionally intelligent managers, supervisors and leaders are way more effective in managing teams, motivating people and negotiating.

They create a more positive atmosphere with happier workers, who are an asset to any organization. Happier workers translate into higher morale, low absenteeism, reduced attrition rate and higher productivity. This leads to happier customers, more sales and higher profits. Thus emotional intelligence is an invaluable trait when it comes to success at the workplace. Whilst everyone within an organization possesses more or less the same technical competency and educational qualifications, only a few rise up the corporate ladder because of their ability to manage people and their emotions.

An emotionally intelligent leader who understands the true value of identifying and managing emotions can empower his/her subordinates with these skills on a daily basis. Discipline or self regulation is essential when it comes to keeping your emotions in check, avoiding panic, remaining calm and being an asset to the team. Emotionally intelligent folks have little trouble in recognizing and managing potentially destructive emotions that can create stress and lower productivity. The approach is calmer, more confident and efficient. Rather than experiencing a more touchy view, these folks depend on their ability to possess a more realistic view of themselves and others.

Coping With Life Challenges

Don't you sometimes look at some people and wonder how they are able to stay afloat through the most challenging situations and emerge even more successful than before? Chances are, these guys score high on emotional intelligence. Emotionally intelligent folks have the ability to calm their body and mind to view things from a clearer and more objective perspective. Their acts are more mindful and less panic struck.

Greater calmness, objectivity and clarity award you more resilience where life's challenges are concerned. Think about the kungfu fighter who can take on the most powerful opponents by constantly working on martial arts skills. Emotional intelligence equips you with those skills to take on the toughest challenges life throws at you with resilience.

Greater Compassion in Personal and Work Life

One of the best benefits of high emotional intelligence is your ability to demonstrate more compassion for others both in the personal and professional sphere. This compassion allows them to connect with people at much deeper levels to forge meaningful relationships. Compassion can be manifested in several ways, including helping someone dealing with a personal issue by taking on their responsibilities or making small everyday decisions for the comfort/convenience of your employees.

Compassion helps you meaningfully connect with people both in your personal and professional life. You are able to reach out to people efficiently, forge more mutually fulfilling relationships and create an atmosphere of harmony and productivity. Emotional intelligence awards you greater compassion in dealing with people in various personal professional and social scenarios.

Boosted Leadership Skills

Emotionally intelligent folks possess a highly evolved ability in recognizing and understanding factors that drive others, which makes them amazing leaders. They are able to make the most of this invaluable information to strengthen their loyalty and forge stronger relationships with people. A competent leader is intuitively tuned in to the most compelling aspirations and desires of his followers. He knows the "hot buttons" of his employees and exactly how to channelize these "hot buttons" to increase overall productivity and positivity within the work environment.

Emotionally intelligent leaders know how to channelize this information for extracting better performance/productivity from people and keeping them happy. People with a high emotional quotient excel at recognizing the strengths and weaknesses of people and harnessing an individual's virtues for benefiting the team.

High emotional intelligence creates better leaders who are able to inspire greater faith and loyalty by using their team's or follower's or emotional range. They are more aware of their emotions, which allow emotionally intelligent folks to create a harmonious environment. Practicing emotional intelligence makes you a better leader.

Did you know that 67% of all competencies said to be fundamental for high performance in the professional sphere is emotional intelligence? Take the example of the world's most successful CEOs. Amazon's Jeff Bezos passionately talks about getting right into the hearts of his customers in a 2009 YouTube video while announcing the company's Zappos acquisition. When Howard Schultz of Starbucks was a child, his father lost a health insurance claim. This turned him into one of the most empathetic CEOs, who is well known showing his employees thoughtfulness by offering generous healthcare rewards. Little wonder then that these folks are as successful as they are. They understand the emotional pulse of their employees and customers to keep them emotionally gratified.

Emotional intelligence helps in building emotional maturity, boosting social intelligence, preventing relationship problems, enhancing interpersonal communication, helping control emotions, dealing with stress, influencing leadership, helping authorities make sound business change decisions, supporting staff and controlling resistance to change.

Lower Chances of Addiction and Other Emotional Disorders

Addictions are generally a direct result of our inability to cope with emotions. People who struggle to come to terms with their emotions use addiction as a mechanism to avoid the more underlying and deeper prevailing issues. When you fail to recognize and manage negative emotions, there develops an unfortunate pattern of dependency on external factors such as food, nicotine, substance, alcohol, porn and the likes. Addiction is just a means to escape from emotions you aren't willing to deal with.

Emotionally intelligent folks are lesser prone to addiction because of their awareness of their emotions and the ability to manage these emotions. They have a solid understanding of their feelings, and do not struggle to deal with it. Since emotional intelligence makes you happier, more confident and balanced, there is a lesser propensity for dependence on destructive coping mechanisms. They adapt more easily to challenges and changing scenarios in life. Emotionally intelligent people are competent in resolving differences and coming up with more positive solutions. Since they display such a high understanding of their and other's emotions, it becomes easier for them to deal with conflicts.

Emotionally healthy people are less prone to be victims of drug abuse or binge eating disorders, which predominantly originate from much deeper psychological issues.

Boosted Employee Morale and Lower Attrition

Morale may be an intangible concept in the corporate world but its effects are highly measurable. You may not realize the value of a high morale when it's there, but you will definitely know when it's missing. Think about the lateness, early departures, attrition, sick leaves your company suffers from. When leaders take the time to build emotional intelligence and connect with their team members, it reflects in the employee morale.

Emotionally intelligent leaders who build stronger emotional ties with subordinates witness improvement in the team's morale, lower measureable absenteeism, a higher team spirit and a greater desire to contribute to an organization's success. The emotional intelligence skill building cost can be minimal. However, the return on investment can be extremely high.

Let's get real here and call a spade a spade. Employees do not really quit roles, they quit senior managers. It is about escaping people and not positions. Emotionally intelligent leaders, who recognize emotional triggers, quickly pick up emotional clues of their team members and "customize" their approach to each member's unique emotional make-up and motivation will experience greater success in retaining employees. This should not be mistaken with not doing justice to one's own voice or feelings. It simply means, presenting an accurate emotional response towards each team member to treat them with greater compassion, respect and empathy.

The problem with most managers who do not understand the concept of emotional intelligence is that they use a one size fits all approach for dealing with all employees, without understanding the emotional framework, motivators and goals of individual team members. This one size fits all approach does not produce flattering results because personalities vary. Some people are more intrinsically motivated, while others thrive on extrinsic motivation. Some folks are quick to reveal their emotions; others aren't very comfortable sharing their feelings. Once you understand the emotional make-up of people, it becomes easy to deal with them more efficiently.

Fine Communication Skills

People with a well developed emotional quotient are more efficient when it comes to expressing themselves. They possess the ability to listen attentively to other people's verbal clues, while also tuning in to their non verbal communication. They know exactly what to say to channelize people's strengths. They use the right words and non verbal signals to help people feel at ease. There is little scope for misunderstanding whilst communicating with a person who has high emotional intelligence.

Emotionally intelligent people are well aware about the most compelling emotional triggers of the people around them. They know exactly how to inspire people to act. People who are able to communicate by emotionally connecting with are far more effective than technically competent folks who fail to demonstrate empathy while communicating with people. Emotional intelligence awards you better response skills.

Chapter 5: Solid Tips for Boosting Emotional Self-awareness

The first step towards developing greater emotional intelligence is boosting self-awareness, or your understanding of your own feelings and emotions. You can regulate your emotions for an optimally positive outcome only if you are able to identify these emotions. Labeling emotions and determining your actions based on these emotions is critical to the process of developing emotional intelligence. When you are more aware of your feelings and emotions, recognizing other people's emotions becomes simpler.

Here are solid, proven tips for boosting self-awareness to get you started on the path of emotional intelligence:

Label your emotions

Label and categorize your emotions. I know this makes your feelings sound like they belong to a library. However, labeling, or giving names to your emotions, makes it easier to identify and act upon them. When you feel an emotion surging through you, attempt to identify it quickly. Is it fear, insecurity, jealousy, anger, elation, depression, surprise, or a combination of these emotions?

Identify the triggers that cause these emotions. For instance, a specific person may evoke jealousy in you because you feel they are more successful than you.

What makes you feel certain emotions? What are the triggers that anger or hurt you? What makes you happy and sad? What is the source of positive and destructive emotions in you? Labeling your feelings and recognizing the stimuli for various emotions will increase your emotional self-awareness.

Grab a pen and paper to list your emotions when you experience a compelling feeling. Mention the precise emotion or feeling that you are experiencing. Accompany this emotional label with the trigger that caused it. What is it that made you feel the way you do? When you recognize an emotion, it is easier to manage it.

For instance, let us assume you feel a deep sense of loathing for a person without any specific reason. You dislike them and can't stand them, but funnily, can't tell why you dislike them. Upon closer examination of your feelings, you realize you dislike them because you are envious of them. You may believe they are always having a wonderful life, while things never go your way. By nailing this emotion as jealousy, you can regulate your potentially negative emotions.

Once you recognize the emotion as irrational jealousy, you will view it in a more logical and understanding manner. You'll begin to think along the lines that it isn't really someone's fault that they lead an amazing life. In fact, they should be applauded for working hard towards their goals. You'll realize that no one has a perfect life. Everyone goes through shares of trials and tribulation to attain success, which isn't necessarily visible to the outside world. Sometimes, it is only how we perceive things and not the reality. Thus, once you are more mindful of your emotions, you can work with them more positively.

Be an expert on yourself

What is the one thing you should do to bring about changes in your thoughts, actions, and behavior? The answer is: awareness about these thoughts and subsequent actions! To make changes, you ought to know what you have to improve upon.

Knowing yourself inside out is the key to being more emotionally aware and savvy. Did you know athletes are trained to identify and overcome feelings before an important upcoming game? This is based on the premise that if you can successfully identify and control your emotions, it doesn't impact your productivity.

Go back and think about all the recent instances where you let emotions get the better of you and affect your productivity. Haven't you let trivial matters impact your performance?

By being aware of your strengths and weaknesses, it is easier to confidently accomplish your objectives. There is a lesser scope for frustration, low productivity, and disappointment. Self-confidence increases your assertiveness while you express your thoughts and opinions, which is important for developing social skills.

Once you gain greater awareness, you will rarely be ruled by emotions. You have a clear edge if you are able to regulate your emotions. An emotionally aware person stops being a victim of his emotions and uses these emotions in a positive way to reach a desired outcome.

Spend time recognizing areas of development to strengthen them

- *List all your strengths and weaknesses.*

- *Take a formal, psychological personality assessment test that helps you discover your own skills, abilities, limitations, and values.*

- *Obtain objective feedback from people you trust.*

One way that works wonders for increasing your self-awareness is journaling. Write in a flowing stream of consciousness about the thoughts you are feeling and experiencing as they are occurring. What are the emotions you are experiencing? What are the physiological reactions to your feelings? Are you experiencing a faster heartbeat, sweaty palms, increased pulse, etc. as a physical reaction to your emotions?

Emotions aren't always straightforward. In fact, they are complex and multi-layered. For example, you may have a heated argument with your partner and feel angry, hurt, upset, and vengeful all at the same time. Write emotions exactly as you are experiencing them, even if two emotions appear to contradict each other. For instance, if you've got a scholarship to study overseas, you may be elated at the opportunity. However, the thought of leaving behind your partner may cause a twinge of sadness, too. You are acknowledging and validating your emotions by writing them.

Dexter Valles, the CEO of Valmar International, suggests carrying a whiteboard divided into two to three parts throughout the day. Add six to eight feelings to the board and ask employees to put a check on the feelings they experience at different points during the day. Determine which emotions have the maximum check marks.

Make a list of every role you play in your daily life such as being a parent, sibling, volunteer, worker, and more. What are the emotions linked with each role? For example, you may enjoy your role as a parent, but you can also be an unhappy employee. Examine every role and the emotions attached to it carefully.

Naming emotions linked to every relationship will help you manage emotions within that relationship more efficiently. It will keep you in greater control of your emotional reaction where the specific role is concerned.

Do a frequent check-in

Do a frequent check-in with your emotions much like how you have a waiter checking in with you frequently to know if you need anything. You do a mental check-in of your emotions periodically to understand how you are feeling at different times during the day. It is a sort of, "Hello, mind, how are you feeling? What can be done to make you feel better?"

Examine the origin of these specific feelings. Are you feeling low and deflated because your boss said something to you in the morning? Are you feeling angry and hurt because you fought with your partner? Are you experiencing certain physiological symptoms as a result of these emotions or feelings? Are these emotions impacting your body language, posture, gestures, and expressions? Are these emotions evident or visible to others? Are you more transparent when it comes to expressing your emotions? Are your decisions primarily determined by emotions?

If you want to be a more emotionally balanced person, reconnect with your primary emotions, recognize them, accept the emotions, and use them for making better decisions.

Use third person

Research in the field of labeling our emotions has indicated that when we distance ourselves from our emotions, or view them more objectively, we gain higher self-awareness. Next time you feel the urge to say, "I am disappointed," try to say, "Jack is disappointed."

If that seems too preposterous, try saying, "I am presently experiencing sadness," or, "One of my feelings at the moment is sadness."

These are techniques through which you are distancing yourself from overpowering emotions to stay naturally composed. You are basically treating your emotions as just another piece of information rather than being overwhelmed by them.

Each time you find yourself experiencing an urge to react to a situation, take a moment to name it. Then use it in the third person to distance yourself from intense emotions.

Emotions don't always need to be fixed

You don't always have to identify emotions with the intention of fixing them. Self-awareness is not about fixing emotions. It is about recognizing these emotions and letting them pass rather than allowing them to get the better of you. Society has conditioned us to think that certain emotions are bad. We mistakenly believe that experiencing these emotions makes us a bad person.

Far from it, emotions aren't good or bad. They are just that, emotions. There's no need to push away the seemingly bad emotions. Acknowledge that you are experiencing an emotion by saying something like, "I am experiencing jealousy." Practice deep breathing for a while until the emotion passes. Rather than pushing the emotion away and, in the process, increasing its intensity to come back even stronger, gently acknowledge it and let it be until it passes.

It takes around six seconds for the body to absorb chemicals that can alter your emotions. Give your body that much time.

We often share a hostile relationship with our emotions. They are believed to be something that is negative and should be fought or suppressed. However, emotions are information that helps us function in our daily lives. Overcome the mindset that emotions are good or bad, and instead focus on using them to empower you. Rather than letting emotions take control of you, use emotional information to work with them.

Emotions are neural hormones that are released as a direct response to our perceptions regarding the world. They direct us towards a specific action. All emotions have a distinct message and objective, which means there's no such thing as a good or bad emotion.

For example, fear helps us focus on an impending danger and take the necessary action to defend ourselves. Similarly, sadness makes us experience a sense of loss and facilitates a better understanding of what we truly care about.

If you move away from your best friend and become sad, this mean you truly care about them so much that you experienced sadness. This is valuable information. Hence, sadness is not a bad emotion. It can be used to identify what you care about.

If you use emotions as information for recognizing feelings, they can be channeled positively. The number one rule for developing higher emotional intelligence is to stop judging and curbing your emotions.

Train yourself to identify emotions based on physiological reactions

Our emotions often have physical manifestations. For example, you may feel anxious before a job interview or an important presentation. You experience the sensation of having 'butterflies in your stomach' before addressing an audience on the stage.

Don't you find your heart pounding with excitement when you are about to go on a date with someone you've fancied for long? Nervousness leaves us with sweaty palms and stiff muscles.

While these are only some of the physiological reactions we experience with our emotions, research has proven that a variety of emotions are strongly associated with stimulating certain parts of the body.

Regular patterns of physical sensations are linked with each of the six fundamental emotions, including fear, happiness, anger, sadness, disgust, and surprise. Human emotions discreetly overlap physiological sensations. For example, lower limb sensations are associated with sadness. Similarly, increased upper limb sensations are connected with anger. A strong feeling of disgust generates sensations within the throat and digestive system. Fear and surprise generate sensations in the chest.

Identify recurring patterns

This can be one of the most effective parts of knowing yourself. Neuroscience will help you understand the process more effectively. Our brains have an inherent tendency to follow established neural paths rather than creating new ones. This doesn't necessarily mean that the established patterns are serving us positively or that they can't be altered.

For instance, when a person becomes angry, he or she may bottle up their emotion rather than express it. This has become an emotional pattern with the person and is deeply embedded in the mind. However, awareness of this pattern can help the person chart another course of action, where the person practices responding instead of simply reacting to the emotion. However, the first step to charting a new pattern is identifying a pattern.

Recognize the build-up of emotions before something suddenly triggers you. These triggers have a predictable pattern. If you are already frustrated, you are more likely to see a situation in a more negative light. Similarly, if you are overcome by fear, you are more likely to interpret a stimulus as a threat. It is therefore important to be aware of these biases and how they can impact our emotions by creating a predictable pattern. The more efficient you become in recognizing your biases, the lower your chances of misinterpreting a stimulus.

Work with what you know about emotions

Emotions are important pieces of data that help you gauge things from a clearer and objective perspective. Don't suppress, ignore, fight, or feel overwhelmed by your emotions. Instead, you should build a valuable library of experiences with them. The purpose of emotional awareness is to concentrate our attention on these emotions and use them positively to create the desired outcome.

Treat your emotions as data that relies on your view of the world, or as a guide on how to act. When you open yourself to this data, you enjoy access to a huge resource of emotions that can be utilized to drive your actions in the right direction. You will know exactly how to reach wherever it is that you want to go if you have a clear emotional route. Therefore, you should acknowledge and recognize your emotions as data, and work with them instead of trying to beat them.

Begin by carefully noticing how you feel at the moment. Observe emotions without judging them or attempting to fix them. Learn to simply notice your emotions.

Be receptive to feedback and constructive criticism

One of the best ways to develop greater awareness of your emotions is to be more open to feedback and criticism from others. For instance, a friend may tell you that each time they talk about their accomplishments they sense your pangs of envy or dislike towards them. This may help you tune into your emotions and emotional triggers more effectively.

Emotionally intelligent folks are open to receiving feedback, and they always consider the other person's point of view. You may not necessarily agree with them, but listening to other people's criticism and feedback helps you work on your blind spots. This can help you recognize your thoughts, triggers, and behavioral patterns.

I know a person who, in a bid to increase his self-awareness and emotional quotient, actively goes around asking people for feedback about his words, feelings (as they understand it and actions. It acts as an emotion meter, which helps him gain greater awareness of his emotions and regulate them more efficiently.

Chapter 6: Self-Management Tips, Tactics, and Strategies

Learning how to manage yourself is one of the most important things that you could do towards developing emotional intelligence, especially if you are within a leadership position. You know that EQ requires self-awareness and self-regulation, but it also requires self-management. In this chapter, you are going to learn how to manage yourself and your emotions, become more focused, and always ensure that no matter what situation you're in, the outcome is always acceptable because of the way that you handled it.

The first step of the self-management process? It's learning to empower positive emotions.

How to Release Negative Emotions and Empower Positive Ones

To allow positive emotions to engulf you, you must make room for them in your life. The way that you do that is by clearing out and letting go of the negative emotions that are currently occupying space. Two strong emotions cannot live in the same space. One will overcome the other, and since it is human nature to veer towards the negative, there must be no room in your life for negative emotions.

The journey to positive empowerment begins now. Utilize the following tips every day, and watch your emotions transform from the inside:

- *Just Breathe* – This is all you need to start. Learn to slow yourself down whenever things feel like they might spiral out of control. Learning to take deep, measured breaths (something you will learn to do once you begin meditating) is an effective technique to release stress. Often underestimated and underutilized, repeated deep breathing in and out will help you relax and loosen the accumulated tension in your shoulders. You can physically feel yourself starting to unwind when you are forced to concentrate on nothing but the air that is moving through your body. With each breath, let go of a negative emotion. Think of it like a balloon, and with each breath you take, imagine the emotion floating away and leaving your body forever.

- *Count It Out* – Along with breathing, you should stop and count to 5 each time an emotion feels like it is going to overwhelm you. You can count to 5, 10, 15 or even 20 – any number that is going to calm you down and stop you from reacting impulsively. Release the negative emotions from your body with each count.

• *Find Ways to Manage Your Stress* – Everyone experiences stress. It just feels like a lot to handle when you're unable to properly cope with it because you've never made a conscious effort to do it before. Things are different now that you are actively working on improving your EQ. To do this, start by pinpointing all the triggers that give you stress and then look at what you can do to change that. Make a list (yes, make a list again) of anything that you feel is causing you stress, and work on eliminating those factors one by one. Stress is a negative emotion, and the only way to get rid of it is to tackle the problem from the root cause.

• *Find Other Stress Relieving Outlets* – Go for a walk, join a workout class you enjoy, go for a hike or a bike ride, find another outlet to relieve your stress instead of just letting your emotions boil and bubble underneath the surface as you try to bottle them up. Negative emotions have to go somewhere; why not multitask and release those emotions while simultaneously doing something that makes you feel good and happy (positive emotions)? If you're prone to being emotionally overwhelmed because you're stressed, it's time to start adopting relaxation techniques. Watch a comedy, indulge in your favorite TV shows, meditate or get together with a good friend so you can have a laugh.

• *If You Need Help, Ask* – Working on eliminating all your negative emotions can be a challenging task for anyone to manage. It isn't an easy journey, and along the way, if you need help, don't be afraid to ask. Your commitment right now is to do what it takes to empower yourself, to fill your life with positivity, and asking for help is sometimes a necessary part of the process. Find someone that you would be comfortable talking to, someone you trust enough to rely on for help. Someone who could offer insight. Surround yourself with people who radiate positive energy – that's another good way to do it. The aura that you surround yourself with will eventually rub off on you.

• *Remind Yourself That Bad Times Don't Last Forever* – Stressful moments and sad times will come and go. Negative emotions do not last forever, although they certainly feel like they do. Whenever you find yourself in emotionally negative turmoil, remind yourself that the storm will pass. That you need to be strong. Over time, you will build up a tolerance and become tougher emotionally as you overcome each storm. The stronger and better you become, the more you will be filled with positive emotions as you slowly begin letting go of the negative ones.

• *Positive Affirmations* – Emotional times can be trying and put us through the wringer, and even though they don't last forever, it can be tough to remember that when you're going through it. Positive affirmations can be your best friend in this case. To start filling your life with positive empowerment, pick a couple of affirmations that empower you, and bring these affirmations with you whenever you go. Whenever negativity starts to get the best of you, whip out your affirmations and recite them over and over until your willpower feels strong enough to resist.

• *Learning to Live in The Moment* – Do you hold onto the past? Has not being able to accomplish something in the past stopped you from getting things done now because you can't let it go and your past failures keep infringing on your mind? Well, you need to stop. This is why you find it so difficult to let go of the negative emotions that weigh you down. Emotionally intelligent people do not hold onto the past; they live in the now. They focus on what they do today to shape the future that they want. They never hold onto the past, but they do learn from it and use those lessons as they make improvements for the future.

• *Knowing When to Take Breaks* – You may be ambitious and determined to work hard to improve your EQ, but you are not a robot or a machine that can work continuously without breaking down. People with high EQ are only human after all, and like you, they get tired. Yet, they still manage to get things done. How do they do it? By knowing when to take breaks. Emotionally intelligent people know how important taking occasional breaks are to recharge and refocus their minds. Feeling burned out and fatigued are not emotions which are positively empowering. Taking care of yourself is how you take the right step towards positive empowerment.

• *Don't Let Your Emotions Distract You* – How many times a day have you paused during a task because you got distracted by your emotions? Where negative feelings affect you so badly that you find it difficult to concentrate on the task at hand? Distractions are everywhere, but people with high EQ have mastered the art of regulating it and not letting their emotions distract them. They can completely remove distractions from their mind when there is something more important to focus on. In this case, positive empowerment. Remove all cause for temptation when you need to buckle down and get something done. Focusing on your emotions never does anyone any good – unless they are positive ones that motivate you toward success.

• *Develop a System That Works for You* – The reason you find it difficult to let go of negative emotions is because you haven't quite latched onto a system which works for you. Or the current system you have for regulating your emotions is not working well. In that case, it is time to think like an emotionally intelligent person and find a regulation system which works. It may take a couple of tries and practices before you find one that is just right.

How to Forgive Yourself and Forgive Others

We've all made mistakes. There is nobody who can go through life claiming they have never made a mistake since the day they were born. You need to learn to forgive yourself first before you can begin forgiving others. Accept your imperfections because you know those can always be improved.

Holding onto your past and repeatedly beating yourself up over it isn't going to change a thing because it has already happened. You're only human, and if you can accept other people for their flaws, you can certainly start accepting yourself too. Forgiving yourself is the simple part of the process; forgiving others is harder to wrap your head around. When someone has hurt us, especially if the hurt runs deep, it can be hard just to let go and let things go back to the way they were. Sometimes even the thought of the incident that happened is enough to bring all those feelings of hurt flooding right back into your mind, even if it is something that happened years ago.

How do you forgive the ones who have hurt you in the past?

- *By Moving On* – We know this is easier said than done, but it is the only way to begin learning to forgive. Realize that holding onto the past is only hurting you, not them. You are the one that is affected by it. Your emotions are the ones being tormented over the thought of it. Remind yourself that no matter how much you think about it, it is never going to change what happened. No amount of dwelling on the past ever will. The best thing for you is just to learn to let go, leave the past behind where it belongs and focus on looking ahead, the way emotionally intelligent people do.

57

• *Never Go to Bed Angry* – This is one exercise you should start adopting every night from now on. Make it a habit to never go to bed again with a negative emotion. It is simply not worth it. If there is nothing you can do to change it, then let it be. Why torture your emotions anymore over something that is never going to change? It's an unhealthy habit. Before you go to bed each night, do, watch or read something that lifts your spirits and puts you in a happy mood. Before you close your eyes and drift off to sleep, remind yourself of all the things you have to be grateful for.

• *Accepting Responsibility* – When confrontations and conflicts occur, it takes two people to rock the boat. While the other person may have had a bigger part to play in the falling out, you were also partially responsible on some level. Being someone with high EQ means that you need to use self-awareness to assess the situation objectively, to be able to see what mistakes you made and how you could have handled that better. From there, accept responsibility for the part that you played, and realize that both people involved were at fault to a certain degree.

• *Choose to Be Kind Instead* – Do you have the desire to be right all the time? Even if it means jeopardizing a relationship because you stubbornly refuse to let go of the need to be right? This could be one of the reasons why you're finding it hard to forgive. Instead of choosing to be right all the time, choose the emotionally intelligent way. Choose to be kind. Being a kind person is much better than being someone who is "right" all the time.

How to Free Yourself from Other People's Opinions and Judgment

Emotionally intelligent people are happier and more in control because not only do they not let their emotions control them, but they also don't let other people's opinions and judgments control them either. Caring too much about what other people think is how you get your emotions out of control. Have you ever been upset by what someone else said or thought about you? So worked up that it was all you could obsess about for weeks or months? That's what caring too much about someone else's opinion will do to you.

To possess emotional intelligence means that you need to be confident enough to not care so much about what other people think. You need to free yourself from that chain which could hold you in an emotional prison. Ask yourself why you care so much about what this person thinks? What significance do they hold in your life? Do they matter enough to you to let it affect you this badly? If they play no major role in your life, why do you let their opinions matter?

The only opinions that you should care about are yours and those from the people who matter the most in your life – like your family and friends. The ones who genuinely care about you will only want what is best for you. They want you to be happy, and they will do everything that they can to be as supportive as possible.

Free yourself from this restrictive and unhealthy behavior by being true to yourself. Be who you are; don't try to be someone that you are not. You are the one that has to live your life. You are the one going through the obstacles, the challenges, the triumphs, and the successes. You are the one that picks yourself up when you fall – not the people who are passing negative judgment upon you. You only get one life to live, and you shouldn't be wasting any of it on comments which don't matter.

When someone else has a negative opinion of you, it is a reflection on them, not you. It is not a personal attack on you, especially if they are not someone of significance in your life. People are always quick to comment on the negative, and this is a trap you must not let yourself fall into. Brush it off, stand up tall and walk away, reminding yourself all the while that their opinion does not matter. Be confident and believe in yourself, and know what you are worth. Treat the negative opinions and the judgment of others like they don't matter. Because they don't. It only matters if you let it matter.

Chapter 7: The Art Of Controlling Your Emotions

One of the first few things you must do for yourself in your efforts to become more emotionally intelligent is to make a personal commitment. Commit to yourself that from now on, you're no longer going to dwell on past emotional mistakes or failures. Commit to yourself that from now on, you're only going to look forward and towards improvement. Commit to doing the things you know you must do to become better.

AS PART OF THIS COMMITMENT, you will not allow yourself to make excuses to justify your behavior when you do have an emotional outburst. Yes, this is going to be challenging. And yes, it is going to require some self-discipline to stick to the commitments you've made. But becoming more emotionally intelligent is just as much about the process and the journey to get there, not just about the result alone.

IT IS about the small changes you make daily that progress you forward, which will help you become more emotionally intelligent. Fix a routine for yourself that works and stick to it every day as best you can. Make it a habit of writing in your emotional journal at least once or several times a day.

ROBERT COLLIER COULDN'T HAVE SAID it better himself when he uttered the phrase success is the sum of small efforts which are repeated day in and day out. This is what you're going to do for yourself now, slowly cultivate habits which are going to help increase your EQ levels as you move forward. Learning to control your emotions is going to be one of the hardest things to do. You're trying to learn how to control a powerful force within you, and it is going to take immense self-awareness, self-regulation, and willpower to be able to pull it off successfully.

THE ART OF CONTROLLING YOUR EMOTIONS STARTS WITH YOU

The art of controlling your emotions first starts with your commitment to change. You have to want to see change, desire to make that change happen. That's the only way you're going to give this your 100% effort. You need to want to become a person with higher EQ because you know it is the only way you're going to achieve the success you envision for yourself. When you commit to change who you are, you're mentally preparing yourself to take the necessary action needed. You're dedicating f yourself to making this change for the better. For a successful and sustainable change, you need this level of commitment.

THIS IS GOING to be what fuels your desire to master all the five core principle levels required for high EQ. This is what fuels your desire to take the next step, to keep things ongoing and to always look for solutions whenever there's a problem.

HOW TO START MAKING THAT PERSONAL COMMITMENT TO CHANGE

Begin by asking yourself why is it important to you to make this change? To develop a higher EQ? Why am I committing myself to this journey? You must be able to answer the fundamental question of why you're doing this, or you may find yourself lost along the way then things get challenging. Knowing your why is how you remind yourself to keep moving forward. Especially during the most difficult moments. When you have a clear reason for doing what you're doing, you're never in any doubt, and you always know why you must persevere.

CONTROLLING your emotions is something that requires a deep commitment from you. This is going to be what engage you to change and to be able to maintain this change for the rest of your life.

COMMIT to learning how to control your emotions by following these guidelines below:

• *Have a Clear Purpose* - Make a focus list of the aspects you would like to change. For example, if anger is something you want to work on controlling first, make that your first point of focus or if it is anxiety, or nervousness, or excessive happiness for example. Any emotion that you think you would like to choose on focus controlling first. When your purpose is clear, you're less likely to lose sight of your goals.

• *Start Small* - Trying to do too much too soon is often how we find ourselves stumbling and falling along the way. While there's a wide range of emotions that you would like to control, start with one at a time and work your way up from there. Once you've mastered one, then move onto the next one. Take it one step at a time; this isn't a race to the finish line. Take as much time as you need, as long as you successfully learn how to control your emotions at the end of the day, that's all that matters.

• *Reflect On Your Progress* - Make time for reflecting and to assess just how far you've progressed. Have your efforts been working well so far? If not, what needs to be changed? Reflection gives you a chance to pinpoint the success of your efforts thus far, and it gives you a chance to look back and see how far you've come from where you were.

- *Take a Moment to Express Yourself Freely* - The art of controlling your emotions is not just about suppressing everything that you're feeling, keeping it locked inside. Suppressing one's emotions is just as bad as being overly expressive with them. Take a moment whenever you need to find a quiet space away from everyone else where you can freely express all the emotions you feel you need to let out. Let it out, take a deep breath, get it off your chest and feel better. Once you feel much better, you can rejoin the rest of the world again.

- *Stick To It* - Follow through, no matter how difficult or challenging it may be. Change is never the easiest process in the world, but as long as you keep moving forward, the hardest part of the process will soon be behind you. Never stop trying to learn how to control your emotions, because it won't be long before you've mastered the art of doing so, as long as you keep trying. No matter how hard it gets, remember why you're doing this and the commitment that you made to yourself. Stick to it and follow through.

SURROUND YOURSELF WITH EMOTIONALLY INTELLIGENT PEOPLE

Success is contagious. If you want to become an emotionally intelligent person you desire, you need to start surrounding yourself with those who have already succeeded in mastering the qualities of EQ. The company that you keep has a way of influencing and rubbing off on you which is why successful individuals always preach about being careful who you let into your life, to get rid of those who hold you back and to only surround yourself with positive, like-minded individuals.

IT MIGHT BE time to take a good, hard look at the current company that fills your life right now. Family, friends, and colleagues. Are these people who inspire you? Are they successful role models that you could emulate? More importantly, are they emotionally intelligent individuals that you could learn from? When you spend time with the right kind of people, you will subconsciously start to mimic the things that they do. You'll find yourself observing their every action, every movement, and slowly, you'll start to include these traits and habits into your own life. Do you know any emotionally intelligent people that you could start spending your time with? Time to start spending more time with them.

GET yourself a mentor with high EQ even, someone who will be more than happy to guide you through the process of becoming a more emotionally intelligent person yourself. Getting a mentor is one of the best things you can do for yourself because these will be individuals who have already been through the journey and have reached the point that you want to be. Learning directly from them is one of the best better mindset habits you can adopt. Who better to spend your time around than with someone you look up to who can teach you what else you need to do to improve. Find someone whom you admire, preferably one that you regularly see to make it easier to stay in contact. Make it a habit of meeting regularly and plucking their pearls of wisdom.

SURROUNDING yourself with people who want to achieve the same goal as you can make you do things you otherwise will not do. Successful people recognize that change is inevitable and that it must take place. Unsuccessful people will begrudge the changes in you whereas successful people will be glad that it happened and welcome it. Remember how emotionally intelligent people are always curious? Because they constantly seek out new ways of improving and reinventing themselves? They never settle, and they never get complacent, they're always motivated to be better. They welcome to chance to improve, and they never shy away from a challenge.

WITH WILLPOWER, determination, consistency, and perseverance, becoming a master controlling your emotions is yours for the taking. Developing the art of controlling your emotions needs to become a part of your life, not just something you do as a once off. Whether you're looking to improve your personal or professional life or both, the way that you handle yourself and control your emotions makes a huge difference in the way that people view and perceive you. Do you want them to view you as an emotional liability? Or someone with leadership qualities because of how well you manage to stay calm under pressure?

Chapter 8: Emotional Intelligence and Motivation

Another important element of emotional intelligence is motivation which can be defined as your personal drive to achieve and do better than before. Motivation also involves the level of commitment that you show towards your goals, your initiative, and preparedness to grab opportunities that help you achieve your goals. Motivation is a synonym for initiative, enthusiasm, and persistence.

The HR Manager of a company was given the daunting task of looking at the company's persisting employee turnover problem, and to come up with solutions to counter them. The lady in question, Marlene, had 2 months to do the needful.

For inexplicable reasons, she kept putting the work on this particular project off. She seemed overwhelmed and was not able to gauge what should her starting point be in this big messy problem.

One day, Marlene had a call from one of her old school friends about a reunion at school. Although she seemed excited at the prospect of meeting old friends, Marlene declined the invitation and told her friend that she could not make it to the reunion. When she put the phone down, it suddenly registered that the reason she could not take on any additional activities was that she felt no motivation other than to do her day-to-day work. She was already drained out and fatigued, and simply could not muster the necessary motivation to do more than absolutely necessary.

The work that was given to Marlene merely remained another chore. What enhanced the value of the work is her own motivation to find solutions. So, in the absence of motivation, a critical emotion for initiative and drive, that task remained untouched in the file, and unless something happened, then it will be labeled as undone.

The thing about motivation is that it drives action not only for yourself, and its energy is so deep and strong that you can motivate others to bring out the best in them.

What is the meaning of motivation? Motivation is what drives you to do something. Typically, all motivations are based on 'pleasure' and 'pain.' We move towards what gives us pleasure and move away from what gives us pain. Here are some classic examples of 'pleasure' motivation that draws us to them:

•   *Survival needs including food, clothing, protection, shelter, etc.*

•   *Accomplishments and achievements such as career, college, sports, business success, etc.*

•   *Fun and enjoyment such as partying, playing, laughing, dancing, indulging in a hobby, the taste of food, etc.*

•   *Curiosity or the urge to know and learn more.*

•   *Sex and drugs that release dopamine, the 'happiness' hormone*

•   *Money which is connected to the idea of freedom and abundance*

•   *Social status.*

•   *Individuality which is a sense of being unique or special.*

•   *Adventure or the feeling of excitement.*

Things that bring pain and drive us away include:

- *Fear of loss.*

- *Fear of the unknown.*

- *Fear of being rejected.*

- *Fear of failure and disappointment.*

- *Fear of uncertainty.*

- *Fear of change.*

Many times, we are motivated to do some things to ensure we are moving away from these pains.

The Source of Motivation

The purpose and meaning attached to every task is ideally the source for motivation. If you are working like Marlene in your office, have you asked yourself recently this important question, 'What is the purpose of my work?' The purpose and meaning of your job is not just achieving sales figures, cutting costs, keeping employee turnover within reasonable limits, etc. It is the ultimate reason why you are doing all these activities.

Motivation does not come from external factors. Yes, many times, we feel the pressure put on us by our bosses to achieve our workplace goals. However, these pressures and stresses deplete our creative energies and are very, very difficult to sustain in the long run. Motivation, on the other hand, is something that is internal and represents our true needs and wants. Motivation helps us focus on the external world to achieve our internal wants.

People with low levels or no motivation are those who are so caught up with the external pressures and stresses that they have lost touch with their internal fire. To reconnect with it, we simply need to rediscover our purpose. When we feel the drive to achieve something, our ability to connect with our emotions that help us achieve our goals increase which, in turn, builds our emotional intelligence.

In the context of emotional intelligence, motivation consists of four components including:

• *Personal drive – reflects the depth of your desire to achieve and/or improve on certain standards in your life.*

• *Commitment – to both professional and personal goals.*

• *Initiative – reflects your readiness and preparedness to quickly identify and act on opportunities that help you achieve your goals.*

•   *Optimism – is your ability to bounce back from setbacks and continue to pursue your goals, and not be deterred by failures.*

There are typically two types of motivators; intrinsic and extrinsic. Intrinsic motivators drive us to do something because we want to or we find personal satisfaction. Primarily, intrinsic motivators are those that compel us to do what we love and enjoy.

Extrinsic motivators, on the other hand, are those that are done to attain some kind of reward which could be in the form of money, good grades, power, etc. Extrinsic motivators need not necessarily give us joy and happiness.

Let us look at some examples to understand the difference between extrinsic and intrinsic motivators. Julianna is a single mother working hard as a waitress to support herself and her school-going daughter. She hates her job which gives her no satisfaction or happiness. But, she is motivated by the money that she gets by working as a waitress. This is a classic example of extrinsic motivators.

Contrarily, John has a website designing business employing 4-5 people. He loves web designing and is motivated by challenging design jobs. He has money saved to lead a comfortable life, and so even if his business goes bust, he can lead a decently good life with little or no deprivations. He is in the business of web design because he loves it. John, therefore, is motivated by intrinsic motivators.

Of course, in the above two examples, Julianna is at one end of the motivation spectrum, and John is at the other end. Most of us in the real world fall somewhere in between the two extreme ends. Most of us work for the money it brings us but also, try to combine some intrinsic motivators to keep motivation levels high. Most of us try to balance our work-life scenario so that we get the money as well as get the time to do what we love to do.

Typically, human beings tend to work better if we love what we are doing. In fact, research studies prove that we are able to handle stress better if we do something that we like and enjoy doing.

Obligation and Emotional Intelligence

At this point in time, it might make sense to talk about something called obligation and its importance. We do some activities even if there are no extrinsic and/or intrinsic motivators. For example, you go to a party despite not wanting to or not having to. It could be because you feel obligated to the person who invited you, and you might not like yourself if you didn't go.

The importance of obligation in emotional intelligence cannot be underestimated. Commitment to obligations is a sign of maturity. Even if you don't like doing something, if you are committed to doing it, then it speaks very highly of your ability to manage your emotions, and get the work done well. To do something even in the absence of motivators calls for higher levels of maturity than being by extrinsic or intrinsic motivators.

Self-Motivation

Self-motivation has many elements to it including:

- *Setting high but achievable goals*

- *Willing to take necessary risks to achieve goals*

- *Seeking feedback for improvement*

- *Commitment to personal and professional goals*

- *Actively seeking out and grabbing opportunities*

- *Ability to bounce back from temporary setbacks*

Let us look at how some of the above elements help in building emotional intelligence:

Setting the right kind of goals – There is a powerful connection between self-motivation, achievement, personal goals, and emotional intelligence. When you set the right kind of goals, then you find the self-motivation to achieve them, and with your achievement comes confidence and the power to help others.

As you go through your success journey, you are bound to face setbacks and failures which will be great lessons in humility and the acceptance that things can go wrong anytime for anyone. Emotional intelligence is the ability to learn the right lessons from the mistakes and bounce back in the game. Therefore, setting the right goals (high goals but achievable by you) is a key ingredient for motivation, and finally, emotional intelligence.

Willing to take necessary risks – The willingness to take risks reflects the ease with which you are willing to step out of your comfort zone to grow and do better in life. As you take these calculated and necessary risks to move forward on your path to success, you build increased self-awareness as you learn more about yourself with each risk-taking exercise.

Taking smart risks requires you to be attuned to your capabilities and your limitations. Even if you take some risks without this knowledge, the outcomes and experience of the risk-taking exercise will help you build self-awareness. So, with self-awareness, you can be better at taking risks. Either way, your emotional intelligence and self-motivation get a healthy boost.

Seeking feedback for improvement – The better you get at something, the more motivated you feel to try harder and achieve improved outcomes. One of the most efficient ways for self-improvement is by asking for feedback to enhance your productivity, efficiency, and the quality of your work.

Commitment to personal and professional goals – Commitment is one of the pillars of success. Whether you are motivated by extrinsic or intrinsic motivators, if you are committed to your personal and professional goals, you will achieve success in both places. With success comes increased motivation and confidence which, in turn, builds your self-awareness, conflict management skills, and finally emotional intelligence.

Actively seeking out and grabbing opportunities that help to achieve your goals – To do this, you must find the courage and personal empowerment. Courage does not translate to 'absence of fear.' A courageous person feels fear, and finds the resolve to overcome it, and take action when needed. In fact, many courageous people use fear to keep them grounded and prevent themselves from being carried away by overconfidence.

Courageous people are emotionally intelligent too because courage is needed to stand up and speak, and also to stand down and listen. Courage is that element that empowers you to take smart and calculated risks and take all the opportunities that come your way to achieve your goals. Courage is not doing something blindly but being aware of the risks, and after much thought and deliberation going ahead by overcoming fears.

Tips to Motivate Others

An emotionally intelligent person is not only self-motivated but can also motivate others to achieve their potential. Here are some tips to help you motivate others:

Listen – Listening skills are one of the most important pillars of emotionally intelligent people. They not only listen to their own feelings and thoughts but can also listen to the feelings and thoughts of other people through their enhanced and fine-tuned active listening skills. So, in order to motivate, you must first listen to what they want, and then show them how they can achieve their own needs.

Focus on open-ended questions – If you want to understand what the dreams and desires are of your loved ones at home or your team members at the office, then you must pose open-ended questions such as:

* *What do you want to do?*

* *What do you dream of?*

* *How long have you been dreaming of this, and why?*

* *What excites and motivates you?*

Encourage – This is the first active step from your end to start motivating your people. Most often, people are scared to work towards their dreams with the primary reason being the fear of failure. You must find encouraging words to motivate such people who are scared to follow their dreams. Tell them things like:

• *I believe that your skills in this particular area will help you realize your dream.*

• *I believe you will be great at it. So, why don't you give it a shot, and give it your best shot? If you fail, at least you know you tried.*

For example, if your daughter wants to start a pet store, and she is hesitant to quit her job (which she hates but unwittingly has converted it into a crutch which she doesn't want to let go), tell her, 'I was watching you with our neighbor's dog. He seems to like you a lot even though I have seen him bark nastily at many other people. I believe you have a way with animals. Go ahead, give your dreams wings. Think about that pet shop you've always wanted to open. I'm sure you will be great at it. You are such a great worker that i you have any self-doubts midway, you can always get back to comfortable job.'

Teach them to dream – Let us take the 'pet shop' example again. You can tell your daughter, 'Imagine that cozy little place that people will love to bring their pets to shop. Imagine it becoming one of the most popular animal hangouts of the neighbors. When you have made sufficient money, you could look at expanding your business to have a nursery for animals to be left when their owners travel.' Let her visualize her dream. The more vivid her dream, the more motivated she will be to start implementing it.

Don't forget to offer help – Motivating others includes offering help. Ask people what you can do. Most of the time, if you have helped people find their spark, they really might not need anything else from you. However, offering to help is a way of re-instilling your faith in their capabilities.

Follow up – Very few people will listen to their heart's clarion call at your first attempt at motivation. If you truly believe in helping people reach their potential, then you must follow up with them, and ensure they make progress. This step is especially crucial when people encounter their first serious setback. Typically, at such times, they are bound to be filled with self-doubts and will need your encouragement.

Motivation is an element that is vital to keep your emotional intelligence high. The more motivated you feel, the more vitality you will have to support yourself and others through difficult times, knowing full well that success and happiness lie on the other side of hard work, commitment, and persistent efforts.

Chapter 9: Secrets for Developing High Social E.I.

While our society is predictably emphasizing intelligence that is more tangible and visible (good grades), the one that goes largely overlooked and ignored is our ability to conduct ourselves in social situations. The knack of regulating our emotions in social settings in addition to being able to understand other people's feelings is our master key to success. While everyone is working hard on their book smarts, social smarts are also vital and, in fact, are proven to be more important than intelligence quotient.

Take for instance, a scenario where you are interviewing two candidates for a leadership role. Joanne is slightly more qualified, skilled, and experienced than Rose. However, Rose has the ability to understand people, works as a team player, and she can also inspire and motivate a team to accomplish higher targets. Joanne is high on technical skills but not very effective in understanding and managing people's emotions.

Who will you hire as a recruitment manager?

Obviously, Rose. The ability to understand and channel people's emotions in the best way possible is a priceless tool in today's world.

Social Intelligence (SI) is our ability to build relationships and figure out our way through social environments.

Here are some lesser known secrets that can increase your social-emotional intelligence by several fold:

Adopt and adapt

Don't fight your instinct to mirror another person's condition all the time. Human beings are wired to mirror the feelings and emotions of those around us. This is empathy! We naturally feel what others are feeling. However, at times we often the take the high road and try to fight this feeling of mirroring the other person's emotions. For example, say your spouse is upset and screaming at you. You know they are angry.

However, you've read how important it is to pacify the situation by not reacting in a similar manner. You choose to stay calm. Then, you try to calm down your partner. This is where more trouble begins. The angry partner feels 'you don't understand them,' 'you don't understand what they are trying to say,' or 'you never get them.' In your view, you were simply trying to pacify the potentially volatile situation. How did it backfire?

This happens when, sometimes, instead of adapting to the emotions of the other person, we try to take the high road to fight mirroring their feelings. Rather, put yourself where your partner is and adopt his or her emotional state of mind. This may help you gain a good perspective of how they are feeling. It also helps them know that you understand where they are coming from, which makes the situation less unfriendly.

Practice being assertive, not aggressive

One of the secrets of being socially intelligent is learning to be more assertive without being aggressive. Assertive people know how not to please people all the time without offending them.

Assertiveness is a reasonable and genuine statement of opinions and feelings. "I would really prefer going to the games this weekend." This is an assertive statement.

You are making your needs clear without being aggressive or demanding. Aggressiveness is marked by a clear lack of respect for the needs and rights of other people. When you are aggressive, you are looking at things only from a selfish perspective or seeking to satisfy a self-filling goal. The aggressive version of the above statement would be, "We're good for the games this weekend."

You are pronouncing your statement more as a judgment without respect or concern for the other person.

On the other hand, assertiveness is characterized by respect and understanding for the other person's feelings or opinion, even though you may not agree with it. While aggressive says, "Only I am right," assertive says, "Though your opinion doesn't agree with mine, I respect it. We can agree to disagree."

Assertive people don't let others take advantage of them and know where to draw the line without being harsh. They know when to say 'no' to people without hurting their feelings. When you demonstrate respect for a person or group of people, the hurt is reduced. Assertive is making your stand clear while showing respect.

However, when you display lack of respect or concern for the other person's feelings, opinion, or desires, you are treading on aggression. Assertive people are unafraid of standing up for their values. They don't shy away from expressing their needs and goals to others. Assertive folks treat others as equals and operate from the point of mutual respect. They don't intend to hurt people and themselves. These are the people who are always seeking a win-win situation.

Aggressive people have a deep desire to win and operate from a point of disrespecting or overlooking other people's needs. They see hurting or disrespecting others as a by-product of winning or being successful. Aggressive folks are more focused on proving themselves right rather than arriving at a win-win solution. They have mastered the art of feeding on other people's insecurities and fears.

Social and emotional intelligence is about being assertive and respecting other people's needs and opinion while spelling out your own needs and opinion. As a leader, one must be assertive to make themselves clear while still showing respect and empathy towards the team. Even if you don't agree with someone, you must attempt to understand where they are coming from to boost your social-emotional quotient along with your social skills.

Here are some tips for boosting your assertiveness:

• *Keep communication genuine and open*

Actively listen to the other person's opinions, needs, feelings, and desires. Watch out for verbal and non-verbal signals to understand them more effectively. Don't listen to respond or react, listen to understand. Similarly, listen without interrupting the other person. Let them finish what they say before you dive in with your take!

- *Don't be guilty*

Don't feel guilty about refusing someone if it doesn't fit with your scheme of things. At the same time, listen to people without making them feel guilty for communicating their needs.

- *Stay calm and balanced*

Even in a tense or potentially volatile situation, maintain eye contact, keep a relaxed expression, and speak in a steady, even tone. Assertive people seldom let their emotions control their actions. They have a good grip on themselves and can maintain composure even in the most stressful situations.

- *Practice assertiveness before a mirror*

Pretend you are talking to a friend who is urging you to do something you don't want to do. How will you convey it to them in an open and honest manner? Focus on your words, body language, expressions, voice, and tone.

- *Always see people as allies and not enemies*

In the workplace setting, think collaboration and not competition.

- *Stick with 'I' statements*

For instance, instead of saying, "We should not go there," try saying, "I don't think we should go there." It makes you come across as firm without being pushy. You are expressing your thoughts without issuing a summons, which reveals respect for the other person.

- *Stay patient*

If you are not an assertive person, it won't come overnight. Commit to being more mindful of your verbal and non-verbal communication while speaking to people for demonstrating greater assertiveness.

- *Respect differences in opinion*

Realize that just because someone doesn't hold the same opinion as you, that doesn't mean he or she is wrong or bad. Agree to disagree and empathize with people even if you don't agree with them. Try to understand where they are coming from and what drives them to think the way they do.

Try to keep a win-win, problem-solution approach rather than proving your point or being obsessed with winning. During situations where you're in conflict with another person, avoid viewing the other person as an enemy. Rather, focus on a win-win solution that resolves the situation for everyone involved.

Practice empathy

Empathy is the ability to put yourself in someone else's shoes and feel their feelings or emotions exactly as they experience it. It is the ability to understand and experience other people's emotions as if it were happening to you. Predictably, the ability to experience other people's emotions and to leverage this experience for helping someone feel better about the situation is a much sought-after skill in today's world.

Empathy is the cornerstone of social-emotional intelligence. By empathizing with people, you can reach out to them and manage their emotions more efficiently. The ability to know how someone is feeling can be used to motivate, inspire, lead and influence people in a positive manner.

Here are the top secrets for developing greater empathy:

•   Traveling periodically to experience different places, cultures, lifestyles, and beliefs is a great way to develop empathy and appreciation for people whose lives are different from yours. You'll develop a better understanding and appreciation of people who are different from you. There will be a keener understanding of why they think and act the way they do.

•   Examine your covert and overt biases. Most of us operate with certain biases centered on race, gender, age, education, profession, etc. They act as an obstacle when it comes to empathizing or listening to people. Make a list of biases that you think you possess and try to read opinions that are contrary to your biases. Look for evidence that challenges your thinking and gradually try to overcome these biases.

•   Nurture a productive curiosity. You can learn something from an 'inexperienced subordinate,' a 'picky client,' or a 'hotheaded boss.' Rather than labeling people, develop a sense of curiosity about what you can genuinely learn from them. This will lead to a stronger understanding and appreciation of the people around you.

•   Volunteer at an NGO or charity organization in your free time. It will not only help you appreciate what you already have but will also facilitate greater empathy for people who aren't as fortunate as you. The knowledge that you made a positive impact on someone's life will make you feel better about yourself. When you spend time with the less fortunate, you develop the ability to understand other people's challenges and problems, which in turn boosts your empathy factor.

•   During situations where there is a conflict because of a difference in opinion, a resolution becomes easier when you understand the other party's underlying fears, needs, and motivations. Even when they are negative towards you, you'll understand why. Watch debates (especially during elections) to appreciate different points of view and understand why people think the way they do. If you find yourself tilting in any one direction, quickly look for evidence that is contrary to your stand. This will help you develop the ability to appreciate multiple points of view without being dogmatic about your stand. At its essence, empathy is about developing a greater understanding of another person's point of view or situation even when you don't necessarily agree with them.

• Practice predicting how a person will act or react in a certain situation by placing yourself in their shoes. This will give you greater insight and perceptiveness into how people feel about any given situation.

• Be fully present by keeping away your phone, turning off your email alerts, and mindfully listening to the other person. According to the research conducted by a professor at UCLA, things we speak make up for only seven percent of the message we are trying to communicate. The other 93 percent is determined by our body language and tone of voice. You are missing important clues if you aren't fully focusing on the other person while communicating with them.

They may be saying something that is contrary to what they feel, which you will miss if you are too preoccupied to focus on their non-verbal signals.

• Smiles are infectious. It rarely happens that someone smiles at you, and you don't smile in return. It the fastest way to connect with people and show solidarity or empathy towards them. A simple smile can boost feel-good hormones within the brain and stimulate its reward centers. You'll do yourself and others a whole lot of good by smiling.

• Address people by their names and praise them publicly. What is it that you heard about praising people publicly and admonishing them in private? Efficient leaders have mastered the art of using people's names while addressing them and using more encouraging statements. Make each person feel important by highlighting their skills or accomplishments in public. This inspires them to do even better work. Even when a person's performance slips, keep referring to accomplishments in public to remind them of their true potential. People respond wonderfully to praise.

• Give specific compliments to people. Your empathy and social-emotional quotient will increase when you learn to be more specific while appreciating people. For example, instead of saying, "You did a good job," tell someone, "The project was very well-researched and thorough despite the fact that the topic was complex and extensive," or, "Would you like to share the inspiration behind your brilliant sales growth concept?"

Be a listening champ

We saw how listening is intrinsic to the process of assertiveness and empathy, both of which are vital for boosting your social-emotional quotient.

Listening isn't only about hearing out what people are saying. It is also figuring out what they leave unspoken through their body language, voice, emotions, and choice of words. Let us consider an example to better understand how listening (or tuning in to verbal and non-verbal patterns) is integral to the process of communication.

It's Friday evening, and after a hectic week at work, everyone is getting ready to let their hair down over the weekend. They are shutting down their computers and getting ready to leave when the company CEO, Sue, walks in and informs them that the deadline for the project they've been working so hard on is pushed ahead by two weeks.

Everyone is naturally disappointed and stressed. The project head sits silently at her desk wondering how to comply with the deadline. The project manager, Ann, says, "We will still do a good job and submit the project according to the new deadline." Another employee, Dan, gets to work on his computer, and few people leave the office. A majority of team members say they can handle the new adjustments. Sue leaves the office thinking like it went way better than she thought it would.

What she didn't catch was the inconsistency in the body language and words of the project manager, who left the office in a rage, while she replied to an email from a prospective recruiter. Other team members went to grab a coffee and were almost in tears from the new found stress they will face.

Yes, no one told Sue how they truly felt when she asked for feedback. So, how was she supposed to know how they really felt about the deadline being pushed? Do you think she was in any way responsible for not understanding her employees' feelings? Of course, she didn't really listen or tune in to what they were trying to convey. She went by their words but failed to catch what they left unsaid. A major part of social-emotional intelligence is to understand what people leave unsaid.

Here are some tips to develop ace listening skills:

• Keep an open mind. Avoid operating with a pre-conditioned, or prejudiced, mind and be more open to listening to people without labeling or criticizing them. I'd say one of the biggest challenges in the process of communication is listening to people without jumping to conclusions. Don't attempt to hijack the conversation or try to finish their sentences. Remember, the person is communicating their ideas, thoughts, opinions, and feelings. Let them freely express themselves without being interrupted.

• We often spend more time planning what we are going to say in response to something rather than actively listening to a person to understand them. Don't listen to respond. Listen to understand what the person is trying to convey. Focus completely on what the speaker is saying rather than rehearsing your responses. Even if something seems uninteresting, listen to it.

- Wait for the speaker to pause before asking questions or clarifying doubts. Don't interrupt someone in the middle of their speech. Rather, hold your questions until they pause. "Let us go back a few seconds. I didn't really understand what you meant by XYZ." Sometimes our questions can throw people in a totally different direction from where they intend to take the conversation. When the speaker is going in a different direction, get them back on the original topic by saying something like, "It was wonderful knowing about ABC but tell us more about XYZ now."

Chapter 10: Things You Need to Stop Doing to Yourself Right Now

Becoming emotionally intelligent is going to involve some rewiring concerning the way that you think. When you look at people with high EQ, observe the kind of positive traits that they emit. One of the qualities you will most often find is positive, and this is because they have trained themselves to think this way. They no longer allow themselves to indulge in toxic and unhealthy behavior patterns that threaten to hold them back from success.

To become emotionally intelligent, you cannot carry around bad habits and negative thoughts. Getting rid of toxic people and surrounding yourself with positive, uplifting ones is one thing – but getting rid of your own negative habits is another aspect you need to look at. Conjuring negative and predictive thoughts in your head before something has happened is known as an unhelpful thought. These unhelpful thoughts and habits will continue to hold you back and prevent you from achieving the high EQ that you want – unless you do something about it.

To achieve emotional intelligence, there are seven things that you need to stop doing to yourself right now. Learning to recognize your unhelpful and negative thoughts is the first step to overcoming them. You are the only one who can accomplish this part of the process. No one else will be able to do it for you. Challenge yourself by now flipping the tables. Drop the bad habits, and start turning your life around today.

Seven Things You Need to Stop Doing to Yourself

We need to understand that much of the time when we let our emotions get out of control there is actually no real basis, foundation, and firm foothold to stand on. The mind is a very powerful thing, and we can easily become a prisoner of our own thoughts without even realizing that it is happening until it is too late. It is because you're carrying around, or you've been guilty of falling victim to, the seven bad habits below:

#1 - Stop Being Critical

We've all been guilty of being too critical at some stage or another. However, this needs to stop because, if left unchecked, it can escalate to unhealthy levels. There could be several reasons why you find yourself constantly being critical of yourself and especially of other people. You could be fed up with someone or something – or your criticism could stem from fear, perhaps even jealousy. Maybe it's even anger and frustration. Your reasons might be different from someone else's, but either way, what can be agreed upon here is that this habit needs to stop right now.

Being overly critical of yourself and others around you can have negative implications. People start to view you as someone unpleasant and undesirable to be around. Arguments are started much easier. Situations get blown out of proportion. You could even end up causing friction in your relationships because of this toxic habit. You know you are in danger of being viewed as a toxic individual when you're constantly judgmental, complaining all the time, controlling, demanding, overbearing, manipulative and quick to anger in addition to being critical all the time. These are all habits of individuals with low EQ, thanks to the lack of self-awareness and self-regulation. This is one habit that you must get rid of to move forward.

#2 - Stop Focusing on the Negative

If all you can think about is being negative, you will never get very far in life. Seeing and staying positive daily becomes a challenge for you. Allowing yourself to remain in that negative frame of mind is going to act like an anchor that drags you down, and the more you dwell on it, the further into despair you find yourself sinking. It will be impossible to accomplish emotional intelligence this way.

Being negative could be something you're so used to that you don't even realize it is your default reaction. Some indicators that you are more negative (than you should be) include if you: find it difficult to accept compliments, always make excuses, react instead of responding appropriately, and constantly find yourself making negative inferences. If you're doing any of these too often, you're likely someone with a negative perception and outlook. This toxic habit is nothing but a breeding ground for failure. Time to put a stop to it!

Positive affirmations can be used to replace negative thoughts that dwell within your mind. Come up with your own list of positive affirmations – sayings that make you feel good about yourself each time you say them. Whenever you feel your emotions threatening to get out of control, immediately whip out your list of positive affirmations and start repeating them over and over again until they sink in and you believe them. Affirmations can be as positive and effective as you want them to be. To see success with these affirmations, you need to make a dedicated effort towards practicing them consistently no matter what. Believing in them right off the bat may prove to be a bit of a struggle, but eventually, it will get easier as it goes on. Affirmations are the key to switching and flipping your mind around, and they need to be a part of your daily routine if you want to experience real change in your life.

Here are some examples of positive affirmations to help you get started:

- *My challenges make me a stronger person*

- *I am focusing only on good thoughts from now on*

- *I am connected, and I am comfortable with people*

- *I am in control of my thoughts, and I choose to be positive*

- *I am more than capable of remaining calm and collected*

- *I am confident enough to overcome all my problems because I believe in myself*

- *I am grateful for everything I have in my life*

#3 - Stop Reacting

If you react more than you respond, then you know what to do... STOP. If you continue letting your emotions be in the driver seat, you will never be the one in control. You will always find yourself making a bad judgment and poor choices, reacting very poorly to any situation that you are in. This will only reflect negatively upon you, and show everyone else the kind of character you possess. If you don't want to be viewed in a negative light, you need to stop reacting instead of responding.

Those who are often driven by their emotions react more than they respond because they lack self-awareness and self-regulation. They don't stop to think about the consequences of their actions. They don't worry about the repercussions, and they don't realize that sometimes saying sorry may be a case of too little too late. Being able to say sorry does not give you the freedom to behave any way you like. Nobody will be willing to put up with that kind of behavior for long. Emotional intelligence defines and determines how successful a person you are going to be and what kind of leader you could make. A person who reacts rather than responds will never be a good leader.

Meditation, relaxation, and breathing are three very helpful exercises that can help you regulate your emotions and keep you from overreacting. Meditation and relaxation can help you manage your stress levels, while breathing will help keep your emotions in check. Meditation, relaxation, and breathing work because they help make the body physically feel calmer in addition to helping you develop emotional and mental calmness as well.

#4 - Stop Blaming Others

Another toxic habit that someone with low EQ has is that they constantly see themselves as the "victim". It is always someone else's fault, never theirs. External factors are always to be blamed; it is either a person or a circumstance that caused them to fail. They are unable to see their own flaws, which is why they find comfort in pointing the finger and blaming someone else's instead.

This toxic behavior just goes to show poor character, and you will never become a leader if you don't drop this habit pront It may be easier for you always to blame someone else rather than accept responsibility for your part in the process, but that does not make it right. You know it isn't right, so why keep doing it? Blaming others all the time just makes you an ineffective person, someone who is destined never to reach success because this attitude is going to hold you back.

It takes real courage to own up to your mistakes, take responsibility and be accountable for your actions. This is why emotionally intelligent people fare so much better than those who lack that trait.

#5 - Stop Looking for Instant Gratification

A sign of emotional intelligence is being able to see the bigger picture. Those who don't have high EQ always look for the shortcuts – the easiest way to get it done. They only seek instant gratification, and they are never able to sustain their motivation for long because they tend to give up when things become too challenging. Thinking that instant gratification is better than the long-term sacrifice is where so many people fail. Instant gratification will never amount to long-term success; it is only a distraction and temporary satisfaction. Sooner or later, you will fall back into that old pattern of being dissatisfied with life in general because things are still not what you thought they would be.

This is why motivation is one of the five core concepts of emotional intelligence. It is a reminder that you need to keep going and realize that every step that you take must be one that leads you closer to your goal. Emotionally intelligent people are not bothered by the distractions and the difficulties along the way because they have the bigger picture in mind. They know what they want, and they will not be dissuaded by the temptation of instant gratification. This is the mark of a leader, someone who can keep their eyes on the prize. Someone who can think ahead and see a vision that no one else can see. To become this person, you need to drop

the habit of constantly being tempted to go down the path
that leads to instant gratification.

#6 - Focusing on Weaknesses Instead of Strengths

It is hard to reach your full potential when all that you keep
fixating on is all the things that you are not good at. A leader
with EQ is not someone who dwells on weaknesses; instead,
they focus on their strengths and the strengths of the people
around them.

Everyone has weaknesses and things they would like to work
on. Even you by picking up this guidebook are acknowledging
that improving your EQ is something that you need to do.
That is already a good sign of progress, knowing that
something needs to be improved. The thing about
weaknesses is that they can always be fixed if we have the
determination and drive to work on getting rid of them.

Stop focusing on your weaknesses and start rewiring your
brain to focus on the strengths that you bring to the table.
List all the qualities that you are good at. If you're having
trouble with this, ask family and friends for feedback.
However, you must learn to accept the compliments that they
give you, and not brush it off or try to downplay it. That's
reverting back towards focusing on your weaknesses again.
Focusing on your weaknesses is putting limitations and
boundaries on yourself. You're creating mental blocks before
you have even attempted to begin.

The time has come to start embracing the strengths that you
have and start tapping into them to improve your life and
your emotional intelligence levels significantly. Also, start
practicing gratitude every day. Gratitude is one of the
healthiest positive emotions that we can feel as a person. Do

you notice how those who are always grateful somehow seem like they are more resilient to stress? Or even if they are going through moments of stress, it rarely ever shows as much as their gratitude does? Not only does gratitude actively remind you of the things you have to be grateful for, but when you actively remind yourself of all the good experiences you have in your life, it eventually helps magnify positive thoughts, and soon, the positive thoughts will be strong enough to overpower the negative and toxic emotions.

#7 - Stop Getting Easily Distracted

Here's the difference between you (in your current state) and an emotionally intelligent person: the latter has managed to achieve the goals they set out to do; you have not. Do you know why? Because you're easily distracted – another toxic habit which you need to stop doing to yourself. While an emotionally intelligent person is focused on seeing their goal through to the end, someone without that same EQ level is easily distracted because they are never satisfied.

Those without EQ are constantly discontent, looking for something bigger and better to come along. They jump from one thing to the next, hoping for faster or more visible results. This approach is never going to work. It is always easier to start something new, but to see it through to the end is another story – which is why you need emotional intelligence on the long, hard road to success. Starting something is always new and exciting, but keeping that momentum and motivation going is where you're going to need to rely on your EQ to help you see it through. When you start a new project or a goal, commit to seeing it through to the end, especially when the going gets tough. This is where your emotional intelligence will help you get through it the most.

Those with high EQ are never quitters, and they never allow themselves to be deterred no matter how hard things may seem.

Sometimes it is hard not to get distracted. Staying focused on a task all the time requires a lot of energy. To help you stay on point: stay focused on your goals, find ways to control your internal distraction (like working in time blocks, for example, while taking short breaks in between), and keep your external distractions to a minimum (put your mobile on silent when you need to focus on a task at hand). Moreover, and most importantly, never forget why you set this goal for yourself in the first place.

Conclusion

Your emotions guide every choice, every decision and every step that you make in life. As your self-awareness increases, you will slowly begin to notice it whenever you're faced with a choice to make. The good news is, you're now equipped with everything you need to know about what it takes to become a more emotionally intelligent person.

As you move forward from here and make the necessary changes needed to improve your EQ, use the strategies, tips, and techniques which you've gathered from this book as you see fit. The tools are here to help you, and you should use them in a way that works best for you. No matter what your ultimate goal may be for your emotional intelligence, this guidebook is here to help you every step of the way.

This is going to be a journey that's going to take time to see the changes manifest itself visibly in your life, so don't get discouraged or frustrated. You are progressing forward, even if you think you're not. Take it slow, pace yourself and don't rush. Take this time to work on strengthening yourself emotionally from within. Practice the strategies in your life every day, and eventually, you will get there. If it helps, focus on mastering one technique at a time before you move onto the next one.

Building and mastering your EQ is something which you will gain over time. It is a skill, a technique and a piece of knowledge which must be carefully honed, crafted and cultivated. Setbacks will happen along the way, but take them as learning curves, a challenge to overcome that is just going to make you better in the end. Most of all, be kind and patient with yourself. You're starting something incredible just by taking these first few steps towards improving your EQ.